Gioconda's Secret

or the Code of Da Vinci

an Essay

by

Pasha Galbinur

RB
Rossendale Books

Translated from Azerbaijani by Gilinjkhan Bayramov.

Further editing by Vincent Walsh.

Published by Rossendale Books
57 Bedford Square,
London
WC1B 3DP
England

Category: Non-fiction
Published in paperback 2017
Copyright Pasha Galbinur © 2017
ISBN: 978-0-244-65153-4

ABOUT THE AUTHOR

Pasha Galbinur (Pasha Ismail Mousaev) was born in 1952, in Azerbaijan (Shamkir).

In 1968 he completed his school studies with the award of a gold medal. He then graduated from Azerbaijan Medical University (1968-1974) and started work as an ophthalmologist in Baku.

During 1978-1987 he studied in the postgraduate and doctoral departments of the Moscow Medical Institute, becoming assistant professor in 1981 and a full professor in 1988.

In 1983, in Moscow, he was awarded membershiop of the USSR Academy of Sciences.

Since 1991 he has held the post of Head of the Ophthalmology department in the Azerbaijan Medical University.

On 12-17th November, 2002 in Brussels (Belgium) he was awarded the Gold Medal and special prize of the Ministry of Health of Belgium at the 51st Global Invention Saloon at the exhibition of "Brussels Euvrika 2002" for his work involving the invention of "Aktipol", a new medicine in ophthalmology.

He holds varuious Honorary and active membership of many academies around the world.

In 2008 (Brussels) and again in 2010 (London) he was elected as co-chair of the World Congress of Azerbaijanis.

Fictional works and poetry:
"A Moon is a Cloud of Hand" - 1984
"Autumn Letter" - 1987
"Colored tears" - 1990
"Like Lost Nostalgia" - 1990
"Medicine as Philosophical Criteria of Poetry or Liquid Light" - 2002
"Whatever was in My Mind Became True" - 2003
"Heavy Water" - 2009 (in Russian)

"Heavy Water" & "Reminder of the Evil" - 2012 (in Azerbaijani), two novels in a 2013 collection of essays - "The Smell of Cognition".

In 2010 the novel "Heavy Water" was regarded as the best novel of the year in Azerbaijan *("Young Writers and Artists Association")* and in 2011 won the national book award.

Tel: +99450 3113656

E-mail: pasamoussaev@gmail.com

The essay *Gioconda's Secret or the Code of Da Vinci* is the fruit of my thoughts, searches and researches of more than thirty years in the field of medicine, philosophy and art.

Pasha Galbinur

Gemela de la Gioconda by Leonardo da Vinci

n the recent Eurovision music competition the representative of Austria, Conchita Wurst, won the contest with a great difference in scores. I emphasize the word "Great" particularly! The musical cradle of Europe presented to us its musical masterpiece.

Taking into account her being a representatives of trans-sexual minorities and her strange appearance ("bearded woman"...) many people expressed their wrath and anger by using different words.

First of all, I think that the representatives of these minorities are diseased from birth as a result of pathological mutation, and as a doctor I look at them as I would patients with thalassemia[1], have the same feelings that they feel. I am very much impressed and regret that they are martyrs in some degree depending on the country they live.

Secondly, I include them in a list of *"victims of the mistakes of doctors"*, because if the pediatricians, geneticists, endocrinologists had made sufficient use of the opportunities of modern medicine to determine the sex of the infant (and not

---

[1] *Thalassemia is an inherited blood disorder in which the body makes an abnormal form of hemoglobin. Hemoglobin is the protein molecule in red blood cells that carries oxygen. The disorder results in excessive destruction of red blood cells, which leads to anemia. Anemia is a condition in which your body doesn't have enough normal, healthy red blood cells. Thalassemia is inherited, meaning that at least one of your parents must be a carrier of the disease. It's caused by either a genetic mutation or a deletion of certain key gene fragments.*

because of his or her external peculiarities in the first days after the birth) by taking into account the activity of the endocrine system, these infants would not change their sexes when they grew up and therefore not form the minorities, who are subjected to persecutions in many countries. In other words just as, for example, clinical death is distinguished from real death due to the benefits from the present level of development of medical sciences, so also the sex of a newborn child can be determined using a modern medical approach.

If a child does not change his or her sex when she or he grows up, and if a male child is recognized and remains as a male, and a female remains and is recognized as a female, then there would be no need for gay parades, for persecutions, or for the protection by others!

In one word, why did Conchita Wurst win the song contest with a great difference in scores? Maybe she won it because the team (or a person) who prepared her performance, possesses a matchless talent in the world in this sphere.

The aim here was to suggest an ideal music from a very authoritative source and to make the population of the world to receive it as the prayer of the Prophet.

To introduce it like the rays of the sun which fall on everybody?

The organizers have taken great risks by providing everyone with the ability to see his or her own ego (man, woman mother, child...) through a performer.

The music was fine, the words of the melody met high standards, and they complemented each other.

The performer bore the image of Jesus Christ, because he is not the prophet of the Christians only, he is the prophet of the Moslems as well. One may say that his prayers satisfy and please all the population on the earth. When she sang, she looked like Jesus Christ just descended down from the crucifix; her internal and external world completed each other. It was not a song; it was the prayer of the Prophet.

Those prayers invited the Moslems and the Christians to unity, to say "no" to conflicts, to double standards, to terrorism, to confrontations.

The singer did not belong to any sex, it embodied women, men, mothers, children, all of them together... like the pictures of Nizami Ganjavi, Albert Einstein and Jawaharlal Nehru made of cloth of different colors, of leather, woven on canvass. No, it was a living being. But it was impossible to touch it (*"Do not touch the music with your fingers"*, wrote the Russian poet Andrei Voznesensky). It was made of song and prayer from the head to the feet.

I appeal to you, my distinguished conservative opponent! You may object to what I say. Can one person embody the spirits of man, woman, child and mother simultaneously?

You, men, I mean the real men! Do you know that genetics as a science has already proved that one of our eyes bears the sign of our mother, the other – of our father? Our eyes embody the positive and the negative features of both sides. One copy in the pair of genes originates from the mother, the other – from the father. The scientists have already conducted an experiment in this area. If we take two copies of the left side of our portrait (photo), the left side of our face, and two copies of the right side of our face, combine them on the mirror by putting them side by side and form two complete faces, one of them will resemble our constructed mother, sister, the other one – our constructed father, brother.

The left hemisphere of our brain has been built on the male (father) foundation, the right one – on the female (mother) foundation. And as both hemispheres rule the organs and limbs standing in opposition, this result in the experiment is achieved.

How can a man looking completely like a woman say that he is, nevertheless, a man?

At midnight when the tired mother falls asleep and when we are obliged to soothe and cover the infant, we become mothers, even more sensitive than mothers. At any age and status if a beautiful young lady deceives us, we turn into a child, even more than the child. *You, men, is it not like that, is it not true?*

Conchita Wurst was a woman, a child, a mother, who appeared in the image of Jesus Christ and showered her prayers on the population of the world, her song wrapped in the rays of the sun... It was the beginning of the road, which was leading to a lasting and grand peace, the beginning of the road leading to unity...

Was it the beginning? No, it was not! As I know, the beginning of this road starts from Leonardo Da Vinci, the genius... ...from the mysterious smile on the face of Da Vinci's Mona Lisa.

As a connoisseur of the spirit of man and an artist of genius, he was deeply aware of all the sciences of his time, he possessed an encyclopaedic knowledge, high sensitivity, great powers of observation and rare memory. He was a scholar, a philosopher, an experimenter who made true and correct inferences from what he read, from which he felt, from what he saw, with the help of his intelligence and apprehension.

His next experiment had taken into account all the tiny details of the problem with exactness inherent to science. In his time he was aware of the results of theoretical researches in some sciences to be achieved five hundred years later. He obtained good knowledge from the ancient manuscripts and sources, which have not reached us, the manuscripts and sources concerning some branches and parts of medicine, to express them in the language of our present day, such as *anatomy, genetics, neurology, ophthalmology cardiology, psychiatry* and others. He devoted his fundamental knowledge to the creation of this masterpiece painting with his profound scholarly apprehension.

With the 'third eye' of his intelligence he knew that each part of one's face belongs to one of the parents. With the might of the Great Creator the Spirit is immortal and it consists of Heavenly Light. It is possible to recognise the smile on our face based on this Heavenly Light (which is in the depth of the human soul and which appears on the face of man from time to time) just as it is possible to distinguish the jolly participants in multi-color clothes of the carnival in Brazil from each other by observing their moods. But it is sufficient in your imagination to take one of the participants of that carnival in dark funeral clothes to a funeral party in Georgia.

Leonardo Da Vinci did the same: the great man apprehended the mysterious smile (I stress the word *'mysterious'*, because the whole world calls it *'mysterious'*) which appeared on the face of Mona Lisa and then copied it onto canvas with his brush strokes.

The most important and foremost objective of an artist, composer or writer is to find a ray of light, a clue amid this great grief and sorrow of life, and to be saved by making use of them.

To create the light of a tiny smile on the face of the deeply depressed Mona Lisa, to make a light appear on her face full of grief as if hidden under the wings of bats, to save his spirit and that of mankind, Leonardo de Vinci invited the musicians, jesters and singers to the feast. They did their best. As a result, that smile on the right side of the face of Gioconda appeared. *The smile penetrates into her right eye; the light of this smile illuminates her right face.* The left eye expresses something not joyful, it remains unchanged. One part of the face is expressive of happiness and hence is smiling, the other part is in grief and mourning. At this moment Leonardo Da Vinci must have felt like a fisherman. When he fed the fish with small bites of bread and threw those bites into the water, the fish appeared on the surface of the water like the mysterious smile on Gioconda's face (it was like a successful experiment).

One part of the face of Gioconda is smiling; the other part is full of grief.

The achievements of genetics as a science, which has earlier been drawn to the reader's attention, explains this strangeness.

We have originated from parents different in nature and many other things; we embody those differences in us.

Gioconda's left eye is the eye of her mother, which was full of grief all her life. With the verdict of God her daughter shared the same fate with her... the light passed through an illuminated door and fell on the mirror.

I am an ophthalmologist. The English ophthalmologist Clive Nice thought that Gioconda was squint-eyed from birth. I want to remind Professor Nice that if we approach this issue with the necessary sensitivity, we can see that there is an asymmetry in all the organ pairs (its reason is known to science): one of our hands is longer and stronger than the other one. We may say it about our legs, eyes - they differ in weight, in functions, and actions. We cannot find a man on this earth whose eyes are equally far-sighted or near-sighted at least in some degree. One may discover a squint in one or both of them when they look at the objective under a certain angle. Mona Lisa is also one of such persons.

If one of our eyes is the leading one, the other one is inclined to be a little squinted if one looks at an object under a certain angle. This state is not a disease, but its reflection, it is physiological and fleeting, under persistent, long-term observation it is possible to discover a certain squint in the person without the application of special tools.

According to Professor Henry Greppo, the right arm of Gioconda is neither short, nor paralyzed. She is simply left-handed. In the portrait the stronger left arm is under the right arm, which is weaker. In reality the genius artist could thereby describe the left-handedness of Gioconda, the weakness of her right arm with real and delicate sketches.

In this portrait Leonardo Da Vinci repeatedly draws the attention of the spectators to asymmetry – to uniqueness, to inequality, the absoluteness of God, to the diversity in the nature of man. The American physicians Leon Goldman and Allen Wordwen suppose that Mona Lisa was suffering from loss of hair on the head.

The Canadian historian and physician Cloud Shinpel thinks that the small knots on the skin between her right eye socket and her nose derives from the abundant cholesterol in Lisa Gherardini's blood, that is, from incorrect consumption of food.

The American art critic Joseph Barkowski, who at the same time is a dentist by profession, thinks that according to the expression on her face, she had lost several of her teeth. He had also discovered that there was a scar around her mouth.

The great artist could easily have erased the tender heralds of her approaching sunset easily visible on her countenance, on her lips and hair, but not everybody could see them. The artist could masterfully and with a heavenly sense feel and reflect the beginning of her aging process.

The low mood and grief of the genius artist accorded and rhymed with the mood of his heroine, the third wife of Merchant

Francesco Da Gioconda from Florence, Lisa Gherardini, mother of five children, who had already lost several of her teeth and the brightness of her youth. According to some art critics, it was in fact a self portrait of Leonardo Da Vinci himself! It is true, he had reflected himself, his own mood, his life, his old age, his inferences concerning man, and he had turned them into an absolute reality. He could paint the death of cells in the human body (apoptosis[2]), which is the beginning of the absolute road of old age, of death, the transition from the temporary world to the

---

[2] Apoptosis is a process of programmed cell death that occurs in multicellular organisms. Biochemical events lead to characteristic cell changes and death. These changes include blebbing, cell shrinkage, nuclear fragmentation, chromatin condensation, chromosomal DNA fragmentation, and global mRNA decay. Between 50 and 70 billion cells die each day due to apoptosis in the average human adult.

eternal one, he could paint the portrait of the immortal spirit.

It is known from history that this textile merchant from Florence had not liked the portrait for some reason and therefore did not purchase it. The reason is understandable. In the portrait he wanted to see his wife as a young girl at the age of 16-17, the one whom he had loved and married. But in the portrait he saw the philosophical world of the immortal Leonardo Da Vinci about life and death and did not understand it, he was puzzled and undoubtedly could not comprehend it.

With his boundless imagination, matchless thinking, with his prudence and profound knowledge in many sciences, with his rare talent and diligence he had reached the present level of development of genetics, genetic engineering, philosophy, music, and mathematics five hundred years before us.

I think that life is a marathon race which goes around in a circle. Those who are in the spot visible behind us sometimes are in front of us. And we do not know how many circles they are completing as they pass on from the spot where we are.

Leonardo Da Vinci is ahead of us for over five hundred years and nobody is able to leave him behind any more.

Inferences

- 1 -

The portrait of Mona Lisa painted by Leonardo Da Vinci is a scientific-philosophical treatise written in the language of colors, which describes in real sketches and proves the physiological essence of the life of man, his survival from death and his transition to the new, eternal world.

- 2 -

In the "Mona Lisa" painting, the genius of Leonardo Da Vinci describes skillfully the beginning of the death of cells in man from his youth, which are not felt by everybody, determining the road he will follow leading to old age and death with great sensitivity and this 'message' has been suggested to onlookers ever since and up to the present day.

- 3 -

This portrait displays the exceptional creative success of a mighty artist, who materializes the eternity of life, the immortality of spirit and visualizes the transition of the pious to Paradise, which is luminous.

- 4 -

The right side of the face of Gioconda is smiling; the left side is sour and full of grief. The smile in her right eye is the picture of man's spirit. God authorized only one person to paint the picture of Spirit by calling it from the depth of the soul. At the moment of death he visualized the possibility of survival from death by holding the hem of the immortal spirit, that is, the light. He showed the road of survival of mankind. He is the only artist on this earth who has painted the very essence of life itself.

- 5 -

The author of this portrait proves the fight of opposites in the body of one man (light and darkness), the existence of man and woman, asymmetry of everything which seems to be symmetrical, unique, matchless, and unequal in the example of man, the absoluteness of God only.

- 6 -

The artist worked on this portrait for sixteen years, yet it remained unfinished. Leonardo Da Vinci did not complete the painting deliberately in order to show that it impossible to be aware of the mysteries of God.

The Mona Lisa - an interpretation